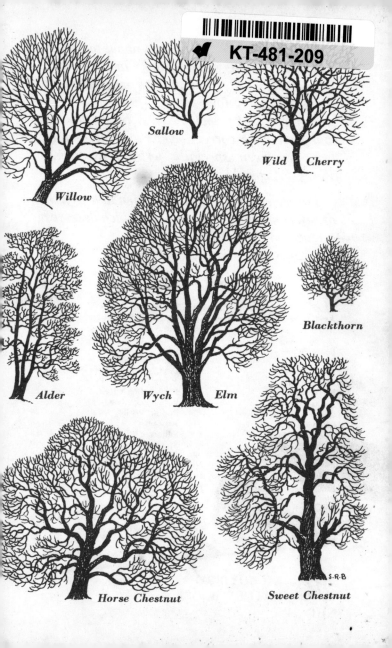

Willow

Sallow

Wild Cherry

Alder

Wych Elm

Blackthorn

Horse Chestnut

Sweet Chestnut

All who wish to know more about our trees will welcome this superb book. In it, famous tree artist *S. R. Badmin* has magnificently illustrated forty-four trees in full colour, and shown details of their leaves, buds, flowers and fruit. The correct, clear and interesting text has been specially written by *Brian Vesey-Fitzgerald.*

For sheer beauty of illustration and wealth of information, here is a book which deserves a place on every bookshelf.

INDEX OF TREES

2/6
NET

A LADYBIRD
NATURE BOOK

THE LADYBIRD BOOK OF
TREES

by
BRIAN VESEY-FITZGERALD

with illustrations by
S. R. BADMIN, R.W.S., R.E.

Publishers: Wills & Hepworth Ltd., Loughborough
First published 1963   ©   *Printed in England*

The Common Elm

The Common or Field Elm is a tall tree with an erect cylindrical trunk bearing a massive circular crown. It may attain a height of one hundred and thirty feet, and a girth of about twenty feet. The bark is rough and deeply fissured vertically, but the fissures

Flowers and Buds

have no definite pattern. The conspicuous winter buds are blunt and are protected by a number of overlapping scales. The leaves are small, rough to the touch, double-toothed along the edges, and arranged alternately along smooth slender twigs. Elms flower early in the year, sometimes as early as February, before the leaves have opened. The flowers are tiny, but there are so many of them that they form distinct crimson clusters on the leafless stems. The seeds are spread by the wind. The leaves do not, as a rule, fall until November. The wood is much used in the manufacture of cheap furniture. The Common Elm may live for as long as five hundred years.

The Wych Elm

The Wych Elm is also known as the Mountain Elm and the Scots Elm. It is not a common tree in the south of England. On good soil it may attain a girth of fifty feet, but it never grows as tall as the Common Elm. The bark is rough with deep vertical fissures, which are usually beautifully patterned. The branches are fan-like and end in robust twigs with pointed, slightly downy, buds arranged alternately. The leaves are large, double-toothed, dull green colour, and very rough to the touch. The brownish flowers appear in March, occasionally in February, and the seeds are carried by the wind. The very tough wood is much used in the construction of sailing ships and boats.

Opposite: *(On left) Wych Elm. (On right) Common Elms.*
(Lower left) leaves and seeds of Wych Elm.
(Lower right) leaves and seeds of Common Elm.

7214 0102 3

The Horse Chestnut

This tree was introduced into Britain from the Balkans in the sixteenth century. The name 'horse' has nothing to do with horses (as horses will not eat the fruit of the Horse Chestnut), but means 'coarse' or 'inferior', the hard red-brown nut or 'conker' being inferior to the fruit of the Sweet Chestnut. The bark is smooth, tending to become scaly with age. The branches are large and heavy, and dip gracefully. The large, sticky buds are arranged in opposite pairs, and each has a horseshoe-shaped scar beneath it. The leaves open early in April, and there is then no mistaking the Horse Chestnut. It can be distinguished at a glance from all other British trees by its very large palmate compound leaves, the leaflets (five to seven in number) spreading out like the fingers of a hand.

The flowers, which may be either red or white bloom towards the end of May or in early June. Trees bearing red flowers are not so large or robust as those bearing the white variety. The flowers grow in beautiful upright clusters which, at a distance, look very like candles: indeed, the tree is sometimes called the "Candle Tree". The Horse Chestnut demands light and so you very rarely find it growing in woods. In good conditions it will reach a height of eighty to one hundred feet and a girth of up to sixteen feet, but it does not live to a great age. Because this is a quick growing tree its timber is not durable and is therefore of little use for outdoor purposes. The wood is white, rather soft and very easily worked, and so is sometimes used for making small articles of indoor furniture.

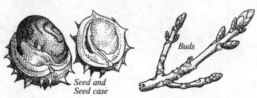

Seed and
Seed case

Buds

6

Opposite : *White and Red Flowered Horse Chestnut
with detail of flowers and leaves.*

The Sweet Chestnut

The Sweet Chestnut is also known as the Spanish Chestnut, and was introduced by the Romans, who loved the edible nuts. Normally the Sweet Chestnut grows from sixty to eighty feet high (one hundred and ten feet has often been reached by trees on very good soil) and girths of twenty feet are quite common. The trunk is massive and erect with big branches breaking upwards, fanwise, into long stout twigs. The first of these big branches usually springs from the trunk about twelve feet from the ground. The bark is ridged and furrowed vertically in a regular pattern, but the characteristic feature of this pattern is that it frequently twists from the vertical into a spiral. The leaves appear late in April. They are long (sometimes as much as ten inches) and lance-shaped with pronounced teeth down each side, and are arranged alternately on the stem. They cannot possibly be confused with the leaves of the Horse Chestnut.

The Sweet Chestnut is about the last of the British trees to bloom, for the flowers never appear until towards the end of July and sometimes not until well into August. The flowers are slender and pale yellow. Unlike the Horse Chestnut the Sweet Chestnut will live to a great age. The timber is light brown in colour and is very durable. This makes it very valuable for use out-of-doors and it is in great demand for cleft-fencing, fence-stakes and poles. Since it bears some resemblance to oak it is sometimes used as a substitute.

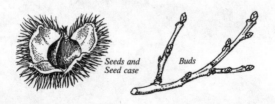

Seeds and Seed case

Buds

Opposite: *Sweet Chestnut in flower with detail of male and female flowers.*

The Beech

The Beech is one of our largest and most beautiful forest trees, growing to a height of one hundred feet in as many years and continuing to grow in girth for many years afterwards. Girths of more than thirty feet have been recorded. The tall, massive erect trunk and enormous branches have a smooth blue-grey bark. The winter buds are long, pale brown, and pointed. The leaves appear in April and are then emerald green edged with fine white downy hairs. Later in the year the white down is shed and the leaf becomes thicker and a darker green. The dark green colour persists until October when it turns to vivid russet-brown before falling. Sometimes the shrivelled leaves will remain on the tree throughout the winter until they are pushed off by the newly-developing leaves in the spring.

The flowers are found only on trees of considerable age, and do not appear until late April or early May. A Beech is at least forty years old before it bears flowers. They are brownish-purple in colour with long, golden-tipped stamens. The fruit is a three-sided brown nut, known as "mast". Beechmast used to be a valuable food for pigs. In some European countries the oil from beechnuts is used as a substitute for butter. The timber is pale brown in colour, hard and strong, and used in the framework of motor-cars and vans, and in furniture making.

To the left of the picture is the Spindle; a small tree which is very common in hedgerows and open woodlands, especially on chalk soils.

Beech
Buds

Male and female flowers of Beech

Opposite : *Beech Trees—showing detail of leaves and seeds.* Bottom
(*left*) *Spindle Tree with detail of leaves and fruit.*

The Oak

There are many different kinds of Oak trees, but the illustration shows the Common Oak, which is a native of Britain. This is a large and robust tree, but one which varies enormously in size and form. It would be true to say that no two Common Oaks are exactly alike in form. The height may be anything from sixty to one hundred and thirty feet, but older trees are, as a rule, more remarkable for their girth than for their height.

In winter the Common Oak can be easily identified by the pointed, many-scaled buds clustered at the tips of the twigs, and by the tortuous nature of the branches, which seem always to be changing direction. Crooked growth is characteristic of the Common Oak, and it is this which causes the wide-spreading crowns which you see on trees grown in the open. The bark is grey and very thick and rough. The leaves open in late April or early May, change to dull brown in late October and are slow to fall. The flowers appear after the leaves, but being small and green they are not very conspicuous. The fruit is the familiar acorn.

The Common Oak is very long-lived. Many have lived a thousand years or more, and it is possible that there are still oaks in the countryside dating back to Saxon times. The Common Oak has played a great part in our history. The Druids regarded the oak as sacred, and later it was essential for the building of wooden warships, especially in the years from the Armada to Trafalgar. In the past it may be said to have touched the lives of Englishmen at every point from the cradle to the coffin. And that is not wholly untrue even to-day, for oak wood has a thousand uses, ranging from the manufacture of hedging-stakes to that of the finest carved furniture. The timber is at its best when the tree is about two hundred years old.

Opposite: *Common Oak—with detail of male and female flowers, and autumn leaves and fruit.*

The Ilex

The Ilex is also known as the Holm Oak or the Evergreen Oak. Both these names are really better than Ilex, because *Ilex* is the scientific name for the holly and this tree is an oak and not a holly. It was introduced into Britain from the Mediterranean in the sixteenth century and is only grown as an ornamental tree. The bark is thin and jet black. The leaves are dark green and leathery, oval in shape, and sometimes spiny. They do look rather like the leaves of the holly, which is why the tree has got its popular name. The leaves last for two years, so the tree is always green; and the acorns stay on the tree for eighteen months, falling in their second winter. The Ilex is a small tree, rarely growing to more than thirty-five feet high. The timber is very dense, hard and heavy. It is sometimes used for cabinet-making.

The Wild Cherry

Three kinds of cherry now grow wild in Britain: the Gean, the Bird Cherry and the Dwarf Cherry. All are usually referred to as "wild cherry". All have oval leaves with toothed edges and pointed at the tip, but those of the Gean are slightly hairy on the under-surface. All flower in April or May, as soon as the leaves appear, and all develop their fruits in July and August. The Bird Cherry, which is more or less confined to the north of England, rarely grows much taller than a big shrub. The cherries are small and bitter. The Dwarf Cherry is even smaller and is mainly confined to the south of England. The Gean, which is the one in the picture, is one of our most beautiful trees when in flower. It frequently grows to eighty feet and trees of over one hundred feet have been recorded. The bark is bluish-brown and smooth. The leaves, when they begin to open are deep red in colour. They then become bright green and finally, just before leaf-fall, turn a fiery red. The timber has a brown heart, which is used in fine cabinet-making. The wood of the smaller branches is used for the manufacture of tobacco pipes.

Opposite: *Wild Cherry (Gean) in blossom and (behind) an Ilex.*
Below *(left) detail of Ilex leaves and fruit, and (right) detail of Wild Cherry leaves and flowers.*

The Crack Willow

This is one of the most common willows in Britain. It is frequently called "Withy" by country people, but that name is also commonly applied to the Osier. Though the Crack Willow prefers damp situations, you may also find it growing on exposed hillsides. The leaves are long, sometimes reaching six inches, and the edges are slightly toothed. The flowers (catkins) are about one-and-a-half inches long and appear from April to June. The branches are very brittle and liable to snap off easily at their bases, which is why the tree has got its common name of "crack".

The White Willow

The White Willow is common along river banks in Britain. It is an erect, comparatively large tree, growing sixty to eighty feet high. The leaves are two to four inches long, very slightly toothed, and are narrow and pointed at the tips. The tree is called "white" because the hairy nature of the leaves gives it a white appearance. The wood is used for making chip baskets.

The Cricket Bat Willow

The Cricket Bat Willow is mainly confined to eastern England. It is a big, quick-growing tree, which sometimes attains a height of one hundred feet. The leaves are grey on the under-surface and this is the best way of telling it from the White Willow. The wood is white, very tough, and elastic, and is the best for making cricket bats. The wood of the female trees is said to be better for this purpose than that of the male trees.

Female   *Male*

Flowers of White Willow

Opposite: (*Left*) *Crack Willow*. (*Centre*) *White Willow*.
(*Right*) *Cricket Bat Willow with detail of leaves*.

The Sallow

The Sallow is also known as the Goat Willow, but most countrymen and almost all children know it as the Pussy Willow. This is a small tree, rarely reaching a height of more than twenty feet, and is common in hedgerows and along the edges of woods. The leaves, two

Sallow fruit or cottony seed

to four inches long, are broad and downy on the under-surface. The catkins appear before the leaves, in March and April, and are very conspicuous with their bright golden colour. They are borne straight on to the branches without any stalk. These catkins carry an exceptionally large amount of nectar and always attract great numbers of bees. The timber is not used.

The Blackthorn

A member of the rose family, the Blackthorn is also known as the Sloe, though the latter is really the name of the jet-black fruit. It is a very common tree or bush in hedgerows. The leaves are small and the stems carry thorns. The branches are often very twisted

The Sloe-berry

and the bark is black, which is why it is called the Blackthorn. The masses of white flowers appear before the leaves in March, and often during a spell of cold weather. The jet-black berries come in October and are much used for making jellies. The wood is popular for making walking sticks. There is a widespread country superstition that you should never bring flowering Blackthorn into the house.

Opposite: *A Blackthorn and (behind) a Sallow in blossom. Bottom (left) detail of Sallow male and female catkins and (right) Blackthorn flowers.*

The Aspen

The Aspen is a member of the Poplar family, and is one of three native British poplars (the other two are the White Poplar and the Grey Poplar) which belong to a section of the family known as the "Trembling Poplars". The 'trembling' is due to the fact that the leaf-stalks are flattened sideways and so have very little stability. In the Aspen the leaf-stalks are exceptionally long and so this tree trembles more than the other two, and its leaves are almost always rustling. The Aspen is a woodland tree, more common in the north of England. It seldom grows to a greater height than fifty feet. The bark is smooth and dark grey, and the dull green leaves are nearly round and are smooth on both surfaces. The catkins come in March and April. The wood is used for making match-sticks.

Male catkin

The Larch

The Larch is a tall tree. It may grow from eighty to one hundred and forty feet high, and the trunk can become stout if there is plenty of room for the tree to grow. In Britain the trunk is usually slender because the tree is cultivated in plantations to form large woods. The bark is rough and dull red in colour. The leaves (known as "needles") are bright emerald green and appear early in the spring. In October they turn a delicate yellow and then gradually fall to cover the earth beneath the tree with a golden straw. The flowers begin to appear when the tree is about twenty years old. The male flower is small, round, and yellow; the female flowers are much more conspicuous, being erect, oval, and rose-red. The timber is very strong and is used for making fences, gates, wooden buildings, and railway sleepers.

Cone

Opposite: *An Aspen and (behind) a Larch in mid-summer green.*
Below (left) a Larch twig showing male and female flowers
20   *and (right) Aspen leaves showing flatness of long stems.*

The Black Italian Poplar

This tree is a hybrid (that is to say, a cross) between the common European Black Poplar, which is the most massive of the poplars in Britain, and an American black poplar called the Eastern Cottonwood. When full grown the Black Italian Poplar has a long bole and heavy, slightly upcurved branches, which have

Catkin

a tendency to bend away from the prevailing wind. The crown is broad and fan-like and the catkins more fluffy than those of other poplars. All the Black Italian Poplars in Britain are male trees; there are no female ones. This is a very quick growing tree, and because of this it has often been planted to form a quick screen to shelter something else from the wind.

The Lombardy Poplar

The Lombardy Poplar was introduced into Britain from northern Italy in 1758. Because of its distinctive shape it is by far the best known poplar in Britain. Indeed, for many people the word 'poplar' just means Lombardy poplar. This is a tall and very quick growing tree; it will often reach a height of one hundred feet in about thirty years. It is erect and narrow, and this is because the branches do not spring away from the trunk (as is usual in most trees) but stay close to it and follow the same upward direction. The timber has no economic use, but, because this is one of the most ornamental of trees, it is much used in landscape gardening. As with the Black Italian Poplar, all true Lombardy Poplars are male trees. The few so-called female trees which do exist (they are not so narrow and close-knit as the true Lombardy Poplars) are probably hybrids.

The White Poplar

This is one of the "trembling" poplars. It is a true native of Britain and is sometimes known as the Abele Tree. You are most likely to find it in moist woodlands, though it is by no means common. It is a large, upstanding tree, attaining a height of between eighty and one hundred and twenty feet and a girth of about ten feet. Except at the base, where it is black and rough, the bark is smooth and pale grey; sometimes so pale that it is almost white. The under surface of the leaves is covered with a thick white down, which shows up most attractively when the leaves are trembling in a breeze. The leaves turn yellow in October. The catkins, which appear in March and April, are clothed in long hairs. Male White Poplars are rare in Britain.

The Cedar

This is the famous Cedar of Lebanon, which is mentioned several times in the Bible. It seems to have been introduced into Britain during the seventeenth century. Though some Cedars have been known to grow as high as one hundred and twenty-five feet and to attain a girth of twenty-five feet, most Cedars in Britain are between fifty and eighty feet high when full grown. Their shape is quite distinctive; a short, stout trunk with great flat-sweeping branches. The largest branches spread out most majestically, and the lowest ones frequently touch the ground at a considerable distance from the trunk. The bark is rough and deeply fissured on the bole, but is very thin on the branches. The tree is evergreen. The leaves are a deep bluish-green, each leaf about one inch long, and are arranged in dense clusters of about thirty leaves in each cluster. The leaves remain on the tree from three to five years. Cedars are usually grown in parks and gardens; you will rarely find them in woodlands. The timber is pinkish-brown and sweetly scented. Since Biblical times it has been highly valued as a building timber—the beams of Solomon's temple were made of Cedar—and for indoor furnishing and lining trunks and cases.

Opposite; *A White Poplar and (behind) a Cedar.* Below *(left) a male flower and young cone of Cedar, and (right) White Poplar leaves and buds.*

The Plane

Spring twig

showing catkins and leaf scars

This tree is commonly known as the London Plane, because it is by far the most common of all the roadside trees in London. Indeed, it is impossible to walk any distance in London without seeing Plane trees. There are many others in towns up and down the country and it is difficult to believe that the London Plane is not a native of Britain. But such is the fact. Moreover, it never occurs in the wild state anywhere in the world.

The London Plane is a hybrid between the Oriental Plane and the American Plane. It is a beautiful tree, which grows to a height of between seventy and one hundred feet with a bole about twelve feet in circumference. The bark is smooth and light brown, and the tree may easily be recognised because the bark peels away in patches to reveal the younger, yellowish, bark beneath. This is one of the reasons for the success of the tree in the bad atmospheric conditions which are to be found in great cities; the bark peels off when the outer layers have become choked with soot; a condition which leads to the death of less adaptable trees.

The leaf-stalk is long, but firm, and the bright green leaves (which appear in May) are smooth with five lobes. The leaves turn pale yellow before falling late in October. The flowers open in June. The male flowers are yellow and the female reddish. The fruit is a knobbly green globe, which stays on the tree throughout the winter, bursting in spring to release a number of hairy, yellow fruits, which are borne away by the wind. But the seed is hardly ever fertile in Britain, and the tree is usually propagated by cuttings.

The other tree in the picture is the Weeping Elm, a beautiful variety which is sometimes planted in gardens.

Opposite: *A Plane Tree and detail of leaves and fruiting head. (Beyond) a Weeping Elm.*

The Box

The Box now grows, in the wild state, only on a few chalk hills in the south of England, notably in Surrey and Buckinghamshire. Box Hill, in Surrey, is so named because of its Box trees, which still grow there in some numbers. But the Box is widely planted as

Male and female flowers

a hedge or as a border for walks and flower beds in gardens. When you see it like this it is difficult to believe that it is really a tree. But it is a slow growing evergreen, which can reach a height of twenty feet. The bole is slender and thin-barked, and the branches long and drooping. The leaves are small, oval and light green. The flowers appear in May, but they also are small and green and not easily noticed. Box wood is yellow and very heavy and hard. It is used for making drawing instruments and tool handles.

The Juniper

The Juniper is a native of Britain, most common on the chalk downs of southern England and in the mountains of Wales and Scotland. It occurs chiefly as a shrub, but does sometimes grow to the size of a small tree. It is most easily recognised by its sharp pointed

Male and female flowers

needles which stand out from the stem in groups of three, and by its pleasant aromatic scent. The bark is reddish. The black berries develop from the tiny green female flowers and in their first autumn are greenish-blue in colour; they do not ripen fully and become black until their second year. The wood of Juniper is too small to have any commercial use.

Opposite: (*Left*) *A Box Tree and (right) a Juniper. Below (left) detail of late autumn Box fruit and leaf, and (right) Juniper leaf and this (and last year's) fruit.*

28

The Lime

The Lime is also known as the Linden Tree. Although a native tree of Britain, it is very rarely found growing wild; but it is planted everywhere as a park or avenue tree because of its beautiful foliage. The bark is smooth and grey. The leaves are heart-shaped and bright green above, but duller on the under-surface because of the presence of fine hairs. They are arranged alternately on the twig, and each leaf-blade is borne at the end of a long, gracefully curving stalk.

The Lime is a long-lived tree, living for more than five hundred years. The flowers, which have a wonderful perfume, do not appear until the tree is about forty years old. They open in July, when the tree is in full leaf. The flowers are a dull yellow colour and are borne in clusters called cymes; each flower growing at the end of a short stalk and then all the stalks joining at the end of a longer stalk. The fruit of the Lime is a small, almost circular nut, yellowish-brown in colour and covered with very fine hairs.

The tree may grow to a height of one hundred and thirty feet and the trunk may be fourteen feet in circumference. The timber of the Lime is yellow and rather soft. It is, therefore, not very durable and is not used for constructional purposes. At one time the inner bark was used for making mats, and the timber itself has been used for many years for the sounding-boards of pianos and some other musical instruments. But the wood is particularly suitable for carving, because it is easily cut and the carver can get sharpness of detail.

Opposite : *Lime Trees with (below left) details of leaves and flowers and (right) the fruit.*

The Alder

Winter twig and catkins

A native tree of Britain, the Alder flourishes in moist situations and is common along river and canal banks. It is a slender tree with a straight stiff trunk and short spreading branches. It may attain a height of forty feet, but the girth is usually between two and six feet. The bark is black and scaly. The leaves open in April and are heart-shaped, dark green, and rather thick and stiff. The flowers appear before the leaves in March. The male catkins are long and drooping; the female short, erect, and woody. Virgil, the Roman poet, says that the first boats were made of Alder. Nowadays, the wood is not much used except for making clogs.

The Elder

Elderberries

The Elder is a very quick growing tree, a native of Britain, which may attain a height of twenty feet when growing in a wood. But it is most commonly seen growing in hedges, where it rarely grows much higher than a shrub. It is very common throughout the country. The bark is greyish-brown and rather corky, and the young stems are filled with soft pith. The leaf-buds are reddish and are not stalked. The creamy-white flowers open in July and have a strong scent. Each individual flower is actually very small, but the flowers are borne in dense cymes so that they form large flat discs. In September the Elder bears masses of black berries, which are used for making elderberry wine. The wood is light yellow and was once used for making skewers. The scent of the leaves is unpleasant to insects.

Opposite: *An Elder in flower and (behind) an Alder. Below (left) Alder leaves with next year's catkins and this year's fruit, and (right) detail of Elder leaves and flowers.*

The Hawthorn

The Hawthorn is also known as the May and the Quickthorn. It is a member of the rose family and is a native of Britain, being very common everywhere. It is often trained to form hedgerows—but as a tree it grows to about twenty feet high. The bark is brown and rough, and the branches very spiny.

Haws

When they first open in April the leaves are bright emerald green, but they darken gradually throughout the summer and change to dull brown before falling late in October. The flowers appear after the leaves in conspicuous white or pink clusters. They are known as "May blossom" and are heavily scented. The fruit is a small dull red berry (the "haw") which is borne in clusters and ripens in November. The berries are sometimes used for making jelly. The wood is not useful. The old saying "ne'er cast a clout till May is out" does not refer to the month, but to the flowering of the Hawthorn.

The Wayfaring Tree

This is a native tree, which rarely grows to much more than a shrub in hedgerows. It is common on chalk soils in the south of England, but is rare in the north. The broad leaves are clothed in a thick cottony down, which gives the tree a dusty appearance. The young branches have the same dusty white

Fruit

appearance. The white flowers are borne in clusters in June, and are very similar to those of the Elder. At first the berries are green, then red, and when ripe in September are purplish-black. They are uneatable. The scientific name of the Wayfaring Tree is *Viburnum*. Many varieties of *Viburnum* are cultivated in gardens and shrubberies for their decorative effects.

Opposite : (*Left*) *a Hawthorn Tree with* (*below*) *details of leaves and flowers.* (*Right*) *a Wayfaring Tree with* (*below*) *details of flowers and leaves.*

The Crab Apple

Crab Apples

The wild Crab Apple is the ancestor of all apples. It is a native tree of Britain, and is common in woods and hedgerows everywhere except the north of Scotland. It seldom grows to a greater height than thirty feet. The shape of the Crab Apple varies a great deal, but the branches are usually spreading and slightly drooping, and the twigs are spiny. The rose-pink, sometimes pinkish-white flowers appear just before the leaves in April and look very lovely as they are borne in clusters on short shoots. The apples ripen in October. They are small and may be either yellow or red. Whichever colour they are, they are much too bitter to eat, but can be made into excellent jelly.

The Holly

Holly Berries

The Holly is a native tree of Britain and common in hedges and woods everywhere. It is an extremely slow growing tree, but it may attain a height of sixty feet. The trunk is smooth and gunmetal grey in colour. The dark green leaves are oval, leathery and shiny, and their edges and the tip have strong spines. The flowers appear at any time from May to August and are tiny, each with four white stamens in the form of a cross. The bright red berries come in October. Each berry contains from one to six stones, which are the seeds from which new trees will come. Birds love the berries, but they cannot digest the seeds and it is in this way that the Holly is spread. The leaves turn dull brown before falling and when on the ground take some years to decay. The timber is white and very dense and hard. Holly makes excellent firewood and will burn merrily even when green.

Opposite : *A Crab Apple and (behind) a Holly Tree. Below (left) details of Crab Apple flowers and leaves, and (right) details of Holly leaves and flowers.*

The Rowan

The Rowan is a member of the rose family and is a native tree of Britain. In the wild state it is confined to hilly woods, especially in the north of Britain, but it is such a beautiful tree that it may now be commonly seen in gardens. It will reach a height of forty feet. On young trees the trunk is smooth

Berries

and grey, but as the tree becomes older horizontal fissures appear in the bark. The leaves are lance-shaped, the upper surface bright green, the lower pale green. The small creamy-white flowers are borne in dense cymes in June. They are very like Hawthorn flowers, but are much smaller. The bright orange-scarlet berries appear in September, and are eagerly sought by the birds. It is by birds that the seeds are scattered.

The Ash

The Ash, a native tree of Britain, is sometimes called the "Venus of the Woods", because of its graceful form and beautiful foliage. It is an erect tree, which may grow to one hundred feet in about one hundred and twenty years. The bark of young trees is smooth and grey, but as the tree gets older

Flowers and Buds

it becomes rougher and rather darker. The beautiful leaves do not appear until May (later than any other British tree) and they fall early in October. The flowers appear before the leaves in April, in loose clusters near the tips of the twigs. They are small and green in colour and very inconspicuous. In winter the Ash is easy to recognise by its hard black buds, which are borne in opposite pairs on the smooth grey-green twigs. The timber is extremely tough and very pliable and is used for making hockey-sticks, walking-sticks, oars, and the frames of large vehicles, like motor-buses.

Opposite : *A Rowan Tree and (behind) an Ash. Below (left) Ash seeds and leaves, and (right) Rowan leaves and flowers.*

The Sycamore or Great Maple

The Sycamore is not a native tree of Britain, but was introduced from Central Europe in Tudor times. It is a stout, erect tree, which grows very quickly, reaching a height of seventy feet in about fifty years, but it does not live much more than one hundred and fifty years. The trunk is greyish-brown and smooth, and bears many robust twisting branches, which are bluish-grey in old trees. The dull green leaves (often black-spotted because they are attacked by fungi) are five-lobed and carried on long stalks. They appear in April and turn yellow before falling in October. The flowers hang down in long, golden-green clusters and appear in May. The fruit is a winged nut, but the nuts (the seeds) are usually in pairs, so the wings look like aeroplane propellers. They come twisting down in October. The timber is creamy-white in colour, hard and strong. It is used for making such things as kitchen utensils and table-tops, and also as flooring.

The Field Maple

The Field Maple is a native tree of Britain. It may be found in hedgerows and open woodlands, and is common in the south of England. In hedgerows it is almost always little more than a shrub, but in open woods it will sometimes attain a height of fifty feet. The bark is light brown in colour, smooth in young trees but usually rather rough in old ones. The leaves are a very glossy light green in spring, but later become darker and tinged with purple. In autumn they turn bright yellow, and are usually slow to fall. The flowers are greenish-yellow and appear in May and June. The seeds are known as 'keys' and are similar to those of the Sycamore. The timber will take a very high polish and is often used for making trinket-boxes.

Opposite : (*Left*) *a Sycamore and* (*right*) *a Field Maple.*
Below (*left*) *detail of Sycamore leaves and flowers,*
and (*right*) *Field Maple leaves and flowers.*

The Scots Pine or Scots Fir

In Scotland this tree is generally referred to simply as "the Fir". It is a native tree of Scotland, but may now be seen everywhere because it is commonly planted, being by far the most important British conifer. The Scots Pine is a tall (one hundred to one hundred and thirty feet) evergreen with a reddish bark, which is thick and flaky with deep fissures at the base of the trunk. In mature trees the bark becomes a pale, glowing red towards the top of the trunk. The leaves ('needles') are bluish-green, arranged in pairs, and crowded towards the end of the branch. The male catkins are yellow and appear in clusters near the base of the young shoots; the female catkins are reddish. The fruit is a woody cone with the scales much thickened towards the tip. Each scale bears two winged seeds. The timber (known as Red or Yellow Deal) is very useful, great quantities being used in engineering and house-building, and as a raw material for the manufacture of paper pulp and turpentine.

The Silver Birch

This is a native tree of the British Isles. There were once great forests of birch on land which is now bare hillside. It is one of the very few trees which will grow up amongst heather, but it will grow equally well in a town garden. The trunk is slender and paper-white and this—with the fine network of dark branches ending in thin drooping twigs—gives the tree a very dainty appearance. It will reach a height of sixty feet in about fifty years, but it is a short-lived tree. The leaves appear in April, and are grey-green in colour. Being so small and light they rustle in the slightest breeze. The flowers appear just as the leaves open. The male catkins ('lambs'-tails') are more than an inch long and drooping; the female catkins are more erect and smaller. The wood is used for making small articles such as brushes and toys.

The White Beam

A member of the rose family and a native tree of Britain, the White Beam is common on chalk and limestone soils. In exposed places it rarely develops into more than a shrub, but in a sheltered spot it may reach a height of fifty feet. The bark is smooth and grey. The leaves are large and toothed, dark green above and fluffy white below.

Flowers

The clusters of creamy-white flowers appear in May and June, and are followed by scarlet berries in October. The berries are not eatable. "Beam" was the Saxon word for tree. It was known as the "white tree," because when the wind blows the under surface of the leaves alone are visible and the tree then appears white.

The Yew

A native tree of Britain, the Yew is massive though never very tall, rarely exceeding a height of sixty feet. It is a very long-lived tree; many reach a thousand years or more. The trunk is erect, but usually much divided. The bark is thin and reddish-brown, and the long branches sweep far out and low

Male and female flowers

down. The leaves ('needles') are flat and about an inch long, and are arranged in two opposite rows on the twig. They are a deep dark green, almost black. Indeed, at a distance a Yew looks black. The male flower is a greenish-yellow catkin; the female green. The fruit is a bright red fleshy cup, bearing a single seed. The Yew berry is POISONOUS. Yew timber is very little used nowadays, except in fine cabinet-making. But once Yew was a very valuable tree, because it was from it that the long-bow was made. The English archers that won the battle of Agincourt used long-bows made of Yew wood.

Opposite : *A White Beam in flower, and (behind) a Yew.* Below *(left)* *White Beam leaves and berries, and (right) Yew foliage and berries.*

The Walnut

The Walnut (the name means "foreign nut") was probably introduced into Britain by the Romans, but it was not cultivated in this country until the middle of the seventeenth century. It is a large tree, often attaining a height of one hundred feet and a girth of twenty feet. The bark is grey with long vertical fissures. The branches are very large and usually

Male and female flowers

curve upwards. The leaves are very like those of the Ash, but have a pleasant, walnutty scent. The flowers appear in May, before the leaves. The male flowers are long hanging catkins. Nuts are not borne before a tree is twenty years old, and trees do not bear ripe nuts every year. The timber is very valuable. Because all shades of brown are intermingled to give the most beautiful effects, it is much used in the making of fine furniture.

The Dogwood

A native of the British Isles, and common in hedgerows and open woodlands in southern England, the Dogwood rarely attains the height of a true tree. Ten feet may be considered a good height, though as much as eighteen feet has been recorded. Its chief feature is its blood red twigs. In winter the

Flowers

twigs bear grey, naked buds. The oval leaves are arranged in opposite pairs. The leaves turn to beautiful shades of red or orange in autumn. The white flowers are in full bloom in June and July. The fruit is a black berry and very bitter to the taste. The wood is not used nowadays. Once it was used for making skewers and goads for urging on animals, including dogs; hence the name Dogwood.

Opposite: *Walnut trees with (left) details of trunk and foliage. (Right) a Dogwood tree by barn door.* Below: *(left) Dogwood leaves and berries, and (right) Walnut leaves and fruit.*

The Hornbeam

A native tree of Britain, though only found in the midlands and south of England, the Hornbeam bears in its leaves a superficial resemblance to the Beech. It is a slow growing tree and never a very large one, seldom exceeding fifty feet. The trunk is 'ribbed' and the bark smooth and grey. The

Winter twig

Hornbeam carries an immense number of branches and the first of these usually grows but a short distance from the ground. The leaves appear in April and turn a bright yellow before falling in October. The flowers follow in May and the male catkins may be as much as two inches long. The fruit is a small nut. The timber is creamy-white and by far the hardest and toughest of all British timbers. Because it is so hard to work it is not used nowadays.

The Norway Spruce

This is the "Christmas Tree". It was introduced into Britain in the sixteenth century, but it was not used as a Christmas Tree until 1841. A full-grown Norway Spruce will reach a height of one hundred and fifty feet in Britain, but heights of over two hundred feet have been recorded on the Continent. The bark is brownish, thin and scaly. The roots are very shallow and the upper ones may often be seen above the ground. The dark green leaves are almost an inch long and each remains on the tree for about six years. The cones hang downwards from the branches and have thin over-lapping scales. The timber (known as 'white deal' or 'whitewood') is very tough and is much used for such things as telegraph poles, scaffolding, planks, and packing-cases.

Opposite: (*Centre*) a Hornbeam and (*behind*) a Norway Spruce. (*Extreme left*) a 'Christmas Tree' Spruce and (*right*) a recently-felled Hornbeam trunk. Below: (*left*) Norway Spruce foliage and cone and (*right*) Hornbeam leaves and fruit.

The Tamarisk

The Tamarisk is a native shrub rather than a tree, which usually grows about four feet high, and rarely more than six feet. It is uncommon except along the coasts of south-western England. The stem is erect and the branches spreading. The leaves are arranged alternately on the twigs and are very small and scale-like. This leaf formation is a protection against salt. The flowers are very small, either pink or white, but are sometimes quite conspicuous because they are so crowded together.

The Maritime Pine

The Maritime Pine was introduced from Mediterranean France. It only survives in the south and west of England, but has become naturalised and now grows wild in the neighbourhood of Bournemouth. It is a big and most impressive tree, for when full-grown it has an umbrella-like form. The bark is reddish-grey, broken up into small patches. The needles are very long and leathery, and the cones are enormous. The timber is not used in Britain because it is seldom straight and is full of knots.

The Sea Buckthorn

A native of Britain, the Sea Buckthorn is a shrub rather than a true tree, though it may sometimes grow as high as eight feet. In general appearance and in its foliage it resembles a dwarf willow, except that it has thorny branches. The leaves are arranged alternately on the twigs and are silvery-grey. The flowers are small and green. The berry is a deep orange colour. The Sea Buckthorn is a rare shrub which grows on the coasts of southern and eastern England.

Opposite: (*Left*) *Tamarisk.* (*Centre*) *a Maritime Pine.* (*Right*) *Sea Buckthorn.* Below: (*Left*) *Tamarisk flowers.* (*Centre*) *Sea Buckthorn fruit, flowers and foliage.* (*Right*) *Maritime Pine cones.*

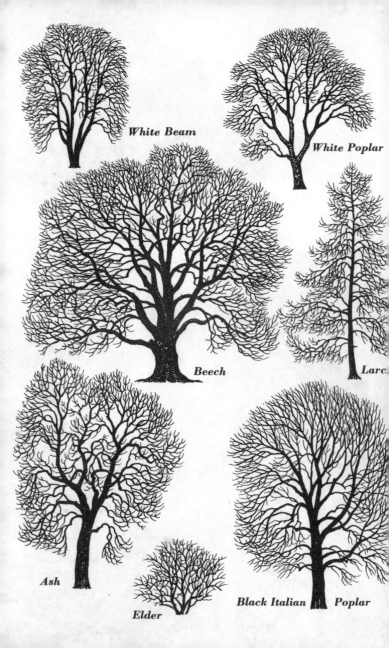